Voting for Spring

Acknowledgments

Acknowledgement is due to the editors of *Smith's Knoll*, *The Slab*, *Magma*, *Poetry and Audience*, *The Word*, *Stand*, *The North*, *Not In So Many Words* and *Writing in Education*, where some of these poems first appeared. One group of poems came to be written in response to a number of short films from the Yorkshire Film Archive, and earlier versions of these poems were recorded as voice-overs to accompany edited footage. I wish to express my thanks to Sue Howard and her colleagues from the YFA for their time, patience and help. 'The Heat Age' was published in an anthology of poems commissioned by the Arts Council, *Feeling The Pressure*, on the subject of global warming. The title poem was influenced by Chris Stringer's book *Homo Britannicus* which tells the story of early human settlement in Britain. My thanks too to the editors and readers of the *Ripon Gazette*, where several poems in this collection first started life. The idea of writing poems regularly for a local newspaper was that a lot of people given the chance will be able to enjoy contemporary poetry.

Also by Paul Mills:

North Carriageway (Carcanet, 1976)
Third Person (Carcanet, 1978)
Half Moon Bay (Carcanet, 1993)
Dinosaur Point (Smith/Doorstop, 2000)

See more at www.paulmillswriting.co.uk

Voting for Spring
Paul Mills

Smith/Doorstop Books

Published 2010 by
Smith/Doorstop Books
The Poetry Business
Bank Street Arts
32-40 Bank Street
Sheffield S1 2DS
www.poetrybusiness.co.uk

Copyright © Paul Mills 2010
All Rights Reserved : www.paulmillswriting.co.uk

ISBN 978-1-906613-16-7

Paul Mills hereby asserts his moral right to be identified as the author of this book.

British Library Cataloguing-in-Publication Data.
A catalogue record for this book is available from the British Library.

Typeset by Utter
Printed by MPG Biddles Ltd., King's Lynn, Norfolk
Cover design by Utter
Cover image: Gannet Strike © Paul Mills

Smith/Doorstop Books is a member of Inpress, www.inpressbooks.co.uk. Distributed by Central Books Ltd., 99 Wallis Road, London E9 5LN.

The Poetry Business gratefully acknowledges the help of Arts Council England.

CONTENTS

8	Brimham Rocks in January
9	Windy Market
10	General Swim
11	Winter Comes Nearer
12	Quiet Please
13	Angel Festival
15	Snow-ploughs pulled by horses
16	The Egg Harvest
18	A Garrison Town Sports Day, April 1916
20	Women in a Munitions Factory
22	Clearing Snow on The Moors Railway, 1947
23	My Parents
24	First Light
25	The Viaduct
27	North and South
29	Travellers
31	Etc
32	High Dependency Ward
34	Blue Football
36	Algiers
37	Caligula's Rules for Government
38	Backstage, King Lear
39	Woman with a Jackdaw
40	Diana and Actaeon
41	Monet in Bradford
43	Saturday Bells
44	Rubbish
45	Beachcomber

46	The Hackfall Dragon
47	The Wild Hunt
48	Wonderful Life
50	Educación
52	21/2001
67	Climbers at Winspit
69	What We Love
70	Lone Star Rider
72	The Heat Age
74	The Fires of Spring
76	Voting for Spring
83	Natural History
84	The Apple Press

In memory of Rene Mills 1910 - 2005

BRIMHAM ROCKS IN JANUARY

Three hundred million years, no Atlantic –
Scotland, America, one mountain coastline.
Britain began with this outcrop.
Silt washed down in deltas of rivers.

Then a hundred thousand years of ice age
whipping across the glacier that shut Nidderdale
storm-blasted the rocks into shapes we know.
Shark mouths, numb slabs,
the shock of cold still in them.

From tropic towards arctic, how far these rocks have travelled.
We walk past where a climber, topping out,
leaves his little trace of blood and skin.
Twigs shake in the almost freezing glaze.

Living up here's too bleak in any season.
We need to wrap ourselves in cities.

Some rocks have holes where the wind still tunnels.
Gaps between rocks
shape the sky that shapes them.
Each is a place where we can get a hold
on the speechless past,
be there and still come back.

WINDY MARKET

In the on-and-off storm sunlight,
torn-up clouds mean a coming blast
of terrified wind over the fields
where low roofs brighten.

Exposed to a battering sky, this little square,
unprotected by its walls of shops and banks,
is full of metal shrieks today, falling tubes
of scaffolding, torn loose plastic and
canvas sails, as the whole market hangs
on its bungee straps, stall connected to stall.
The weather is useless to sellers of Chinese-style
handbags, fine bone china mugs, luxury
All-Season feather duvets,
a T-shirt with a flaming skull.

Here once street lamps glowed with sewer gas,
wives were sold at auction, convicts leaving for
Botany Bay felt their nervous bones rattle
in irons somewhere by the taxi stand;
somebody whispered a name he loves,
the brand-wound still hot.

Now, in the new century, in this wind
while the sky darkens, while things fall
steadily apart, I imagine the market,
in some strange hook-up with the weather,
nothing to hold it to the ground,
a diminishing, striped, trestle-tabled assemblage,
scattering knives, CDs, cassettes and flowers,
becoming now a single sail higher and higher in the air,
as it twists with a flap out of sight.

GENERAL SWIM

Morning's first swimmers curl their toes
at the edge of a huge green cube, ice-still,
but getting in, it's lukewarm.
Voices are one molten shout, lasting
all day in the wriggling green-tiled water.

Floating grins, bubble-blowing lips, legs
with a sudden kick in them. A big pink starfish
hangs suspended in the shape of a child,
bobs up like a cork as far as the air. A tiny thing
called Harriet with luminous arm-bands
has drifted out of the shallow end.

                    On my back,
I watch the sliding plaster ceiling, texture
of cellulite or old custard, nothing to support it.
A scream, echo-prolonged, pierces my eyeball
with somebody's joy. Kids with fists like grenades
slam the surface. This is the crawl.

Shoulders grow heavier over the years.
Bodies of the young lengthen like shadows.
And now in mid afternoon, late August,
the sun finds a space between trees through a window,
shines direct on water, covers a wall with ripples
of dazzle, a high-speed light-storm of shimmering.

Outside, people enter a brightness,
a shivery feeling between clothes and skin.
There's a strange colour in the air,
in their gaze as they move, a damp glistening,
each an ounce or two lighter, a splash happier.

WINTER COMES NEARER

On Hallowe'en, a young girl looks in a mirror.
Bite an apple, her friends tell her for a dare,
and behind your shoulder you'll see the face
of the love of your life. Or if it's nobody, a skull.

A few nights later, bonfires are lit.
Our whole town gathers
on a hill where a fiery dragon
blows sparks at stars and melts the moon.

Parents, grandparents, children, their friends,
every Novermber for four hundred years
watch Guy Fawkes as a torrent
of flames pulls him slowly apart.

The sky fills up with roses, dazzling
blossoms, shrieking explosions.
Silver was never so silver or blue so blue.
Colour squirts through the air at the end of a stick.

We stare into scenes tracing
the flying curves of the Sydney Opera House in light,
in tropical-eyed peacock feathers,
as if the entire conspiracy

happened so that in starlight and mud
this firework would pour its demonic blue,
these go cannoning over the crowd,
this one's feelers of brilliance spiral orange.

Afterwards, when the barrage has stopped,
we catch our first glimpse of winter in the
gunpowder-grey forest of these wriggling away
smoke-trails, its branches thick as frost.

QUIET PLEASE

Crime, Romance, Fiction, History,
Pets, Computers, Cookery, Religion,
Ghosts in Yorkshire. Listed, alphabetical.

Decency at the Helpdesk. Laughter
at Customer Information. Clicking of mice.
Tapping of keys. Folding and flattening
of newspapers. Unwrapping of illegal sweets.

The spider-lilies and monsteras are glossy,
the parlour palms watered. Items on loan,
checked in or late. The till rings. It's a fine
Through a window yesterday's slush freezes.

The old library at the bottom of the hill
is derelict now, exposed to damp and its stained doings,
shelves like useless scenery. In one room
a collection of burned-out candles, a place
to meet in secret. Maybe kids come here.

There's a smell of neglect. Slits of light
live with the long silence of nothing doing, no voices
only the street, frightening ordinary rain on a skylight, traffic.
We like places clean, cared for, part of everybody's day,
owned, and hate raw cold, decay, thick dust and slush
of broken glass, the outside coming in.

ANGEL FESTIVAL

You can make the body of an angel
with fifty light bulbs, chicken wire,
carrier bags, plastic bottles.

With a whole school's worth
of cut-out paper hands you can make wings.
An angel is holding a book which shows
the names of the children who made it.

If these fly, they're invisible,
pound the air like swans, then stand
wings folded, never seem out of breath.

As for the real angels,
you were just minding your sheep that night
when out of the stars…
Their singing disembowels you with joy.

The trumpets of angels brought down the walls of a city.
You were shot through with a single blast.
There were angels who shut the mouths of the lions.
You are still alive, a walking miracle.

They come in swarms, stinging you with bliss.
Ten thousand times ten thousand.
They are the humming in the garden.

I saw a meccano angel, an angel
with a lampshade for a head like a huge moth,
an angel made of clustering blue butterflies.

I saw an earwig crawl on the furry sleeve
of the angel in the Oxfam window.
Even the marble and granite angels

in the stone mason's looked unusual.

An angel's face is the most difficult thing.
What expression can you have
if you were with God from the beginning?

After a while we are seeing angels everywhere.
One is sitting peacefully in a tree, wings folded.
This little housefly is a messenger of God.

SNOW-PLOUGHS PULLED BY HORSES

1908, streets by the Midland Station,
horses led by men in ash-grey light.
Tails swish, snow-ploughs gather weight.
The spine of every horse strains forward.

Without horses, snow-ploughs, men,
there'd be no movement, only places
empty this morning, squares
and statues outlined in thick cold,

time of day when fires are lit in rooms
down streets buried in deep silence.
Yet someone with a camera sees
this moment's movement,

follows and sees where snow is piled
like hayricks or soiled laundry,
into carts like corpses. So the day
begins with work, moves forward –

snow, grey from its fall through grey air,
from miles of sky over Slack, Chisley,
emptied into the sewers of Bradford,
its last journey just hours from its first.

THE EGG HARVEST

Stuff to carry, rope, pulleys, spades,
nobody looks at the camera,
a handle turning jerkily

by which we follow every move
just as it happened in 1908 at Flamborough
but without voices, bird cries, thud of the tide.

Chalk, a hundred million years old,
the same under the plains of Northern France,
shows a place where men manage equipment.

One looped in a rope paid to the edge.
His feet recognize the drop.

We watch him slither towards it,
the one who'll bring back the prize,
who goes down into sheer space
as waves rise and shatter.

He's wearing a battered steel helmet,
one with its spike missing – military junk.

Afternoon turns the sea milky with shadows.
He swings to the cliff with fingers stretched
towards eggs of gannets, fulmars,
as in a larder or the shelf of a tomb.

Swings to crush (look out mind it)
such new-laid envelopes of shell
in the big pocket of his poacher's jacket.

They hold him like a fob-watch on a chain,
hear his shout, *Get me up now lads*, so they do,
heave by heave like rowers in a skiff.

He brings them a white spring harvest,
shared on the grass to sell in full baskets,
each oval a hell of half-generation.

Then for our entertainment
a guillemot and a puffin captured alive,
grasped in either hand.

He makes them seem to fly up and down, up down,
each sharply-weaponed face
stabbing the other in a kind of embrace
right at the camera.

No No No we shout from the incredible future.

A GARRISON TOWN SPORTS DAY, APRIL 1916

Soldiers from the camp and townspeople
mixed up behind wire in a crowd together
stand about on a cold spring afternoon
blocking our view of what surrounds them
racecourse grass and neutral sky.

The camera rolls across them and moves on,
faces framed by faces.
Instant footage shrinks them to the moment,
the big picture happening somewhere else
in this year of the Somme.
We notice what we can before it passes
how the cold rubs hands together
keeps them tapping cigarettes.

Boys among towers of men;
girls and women, sisters, wives
snuggled inside buttoned battered coats;
everyone in uniform of a sort
just comfortable under their angled hats.

Glum, flirtatious, gentle, gaunt,
out for a skulk, a gallivant, a caper,
one gives a victory sign, another's about to sneeze
though we won't hear it, see only tassels
of regiment caps flying, cigarette smoke in the wind.

We watch them face to face
nine weeks to the killing season
as they're shown a practice demonstration,
bayonets unzipping sacks like bodies on the grass,
but it's alright; a figure in a bowler hat, Chaplin-style
comes clowning; horses bound for Thiepval, Ovillers

gallop over fences in a drowse; a piper plays
as legs in a kilt hopscotch between crossed swords.

Past a glittering corner of lake
first of the runners make it back,
(how skinny they look) into the straight,
to cheers, maybe a far-flung shout.

All winners, they're together now for a photograph
still with energy left, and laughing so we catch
the high-up thrown, hats-off-to-everything pitch
of voices almost getting through, in thinnest traces.

The crowd make silly faces: a happy music hall stand-up
audience, jostling for a view, and soon they'll be on view
in the town cinema, 'That's me, there's you, see her'!

We hear them, or think we can
under a blank chilly April sky
before the long summer silence.

WOMEN IN A MUNITIONS FACTORY

See us in overalls rolling these with our feet. *Softs*
we call them, great long cigar-looking things.
Eighty five pound shells they come out as.

This is the day they filmed us, made it look easy,
as if levers and pulleys do it,
not like when one clocks you round your nut.

On cranes and lathes,
turners and polishers, bare-armed drillers.
Shopping queues, the family wash. Then *this!*

A girl unloads them one by one from the fire,
gloved hands and a rag, one end molten. Next time
it'll glow this white's in Libya or somewhere.

Which is me? Her in goggles? That one in high heels?
I hear myself think, *The more we make –
the quicker he'll be back.*

Today their majesties are visiting.
We stand in a line, curtsey.
The gaffer looks at his watch.

When the invasion comes you have to
listen for peals of bells dead of night.

What will people think of us – in fifty years,
a hundred, knowing what we don't?

Sometimes I lie in the dark.
I can't see anything, hear anything.
What's happening to me?
What am I turning into?

On my way to work I feel alright –
Mrs Southern's tulips,
her fence freshly creosoted.

We knock off before teatime to get home.
It's sunny today. Groups of us in the street.
You can see me there, shading my eyes.

CLEARING SNOW ON THE MOORS RAILWAY, 1947

Catching our death for the Great North Eastern,
what choice was there? Factory, office,
schoolteaching, shop, your arse on the line,
Huntley and Palmer, Glori-tone. Give me disaster.

But picks and spades in snow this thick?
Might as well try pissing holes
in the Great Wall of China.
Scarves, boots, uniforms,
look at them, standing knackered,
like they'd just been shot but hadn't dropped.

'Why don't you just fuck off then',
I say to one who thinks he's clever,
'On you go! Fuck off back to
Wallpaperland, Biscuitfactoryshire'.

Shovelling ice that grips the track,
drifts, some of them house-wall high,
nobody knows if it's for England
or GNER his eyes freeze over.

If there's men and work to do, let's do it.
Splash petrol, set it alight. Snow burns!
Get an ice-plough, drive it hard
through chunks of Arctic. Then our best invention,
a jet engine, aimed from a truck at walking pace.
Ice, muck, cinders fly. The cold surrenders.

MY PARENTS

1940, married a year, stopping in front of a camera
outside a church at his brother's wedding.
His shoes still in their morning polish in the rain.
Hers laced-up, high-heeled. His stuck out
under his trouser folds, buttoned jacket slightly too small
even for his sparrow-shouldered frame.
Worsted trousers ironed all the way up. Her right hand tucked
above his elbow, handbag in her left gloved hand.
Five white roses pinned to her zig-zag lapel. Above his parting,
two Victorian semis hazy with firesmoke
blowing into a street by the cemetery wall.
Behind them three black stumps of a lime
cut back by the photograph's white mount.
At her left padded shoulder a gravestone. Their faces small,
smiling, caught in the morning, drizzled into,
part of the day, together in it, lips parted,
a handkerchief wedged, white under his rose.
A straightness in him. Over her womb the pockets
on her jacket closed like lids. A day on its way
to celebrations, laughter. A happy moment.
The war like a puddle of sky just to his right,
still months to Dunkirk, unruffled, blank –
an offside mirror. She beside him, waiting for the aperture
to click, for the moment to be returned to movement,
waiting – she didn't know it –
for her first pregnancies-to-be, each one lost,
each attached to a fading dawn star,
eight years for a child to be actually born,
who looks now at a riddle, at a miracle
solid as creased cloth, leather polish –
coats, flowers, shoes, lips, no story,
only where they walked and stopped, moved on.

FIRST LIGHT

My mother never reached this point
before, finished the journey. Before,
it ended abruptly, bloodily.

There had been twins and a little girl.
No more than shadowy marks
on a cave wall. I had come later

to a place where their ghosts
were still part of the rock, just a glisten
of animal presence, in a corner

of my unopened eyes.
I missed them somewhere.
I was there, trying to become human,

while the trees outside her window
broke into blossom And then,
finding the sunshine they never found –

those others, half beast, half stone,
my little sister, brother and sister –
I came out, and here all this is.

THE VIADUCT

Lovers under the arch by the empty henhouses,
echoes under the brick arch by the cemetery.
Smoke abandoned on the long inclined crawl
of trains towards the station.

Three women walking the road by the river.
My mother and her sisters singing to me
a week before I was born – What I heard
under their songs was vibration, movement
of steel up-line to the engineering works.

        *

Smoke incandescent from furnaces
flying straight through the night
to Manchester, Sheffield, Leeds.
Black stone was half our sky.

Church-bells, skylarks, small crowd football shouts,
and a terrible grinding (*WORK   WORK*
uphill, under steam, smoke in the grass)
of a world getting heavier.

Daring to walk its length once, I leaned out
over a low barrier, looking down
on safe gardens, havens with garages,
then streets by the cricket field, doors off hinges,
cars on piles of brick. A plumb drop
into the oil-skimmed river. Arch by arch
nearly a mile, town on one side,
fields the other; beyond, the hills
where the Green Knight sharpened his axe,
industrial country even in the fourteenth century.

*

Now, after forty years,
I come back, and am standing
under the helm of a leaky arch
slippery with echoes, remains
of a growing bush half-way up,
ivy underfoot, a path – sort of – through litter.

The stone hardly trembles when a two-coach commuter train
crosses at the speed of nonchalance.

*

It seems I owe it something, for being there so long,
what it cost in scale, management, deaths probably.
Its shape leans in the sun
on the backs of house-walls,
over the main road, our lives too,
unknowingly shadowed.

I see its whole structure as a design,
arch behind arch to a horizon, as if somewhere
it must shrink to nothing, end its story –
all that lifting of gear, chained enterprise,
weekly discussions of homework sheltering from rain,
what it protected, what stayed hidden

NORTH AND SOUTH

From salt flats, chemical works, reading the map
from the back seat of our Morris, Cheshire into Shropshire
south south, the car window a screen, England showing.

From scars and scarps, land depressed by ice,
to spinneys and heaths, fields full of the stillness
of growing wheat, to where chalk flowed, heat whispered,
early July evenings shone like glaze.

The road ran close to hedgerows, but there was a summer
closer than anything seen or reached by roads.
Sometimes we stopped, wandered into it, couldn't find it again,
then it was there, an Oxfordshire school house garden,
line of pollarded willows, opaque heavy centrifugal elms.

Tewkesbury, Cirencester, Chippenham, Melksham,
a white horse on a hill kept pace with us, veered off,
none following it (or could we?), back to prehistory.

In folds of chalk, in hints of caves, the sea reached us
long before its cliffs stood out white.
By Blandford we were immersed.

We should have known these milky streams,
this Avebury of the mind was an illusion.
Melksham aspired the same way as Warrington.
Half the country, as we headed south,
was travelling north, trying to become Manchester.

When we reached Purbeck, my mother covered her white feet
with the tide, at home with the illusion, the air soft like lint.
At Dancing Ledge the waves ran in and in,
after a million summers of warm rock.

We'd got as far as we could, yet we came back, year after year,
looking for a way though, for that fold in the cliff, in the geology
where there was no Stockport, no journey,
no ticking fan-belt, just grass, just thrift.

TRAVELLERS

My son visits my mother in her care home.
She manages with help down the corridor,
just manages to speak but listening's easier.
He's telling her about his plans, his friends
travelling with him to Peru, Bolivia,
New Zealand, India, Nepal.

He holds her hand. He'll see her again soon.
We've pulled up a couple of chairs next to her chair.
In the room the people, all women,
are arguing about whether it's Saturday or Sunday.
It's Sunday. Most of the day they sleep like old pets,
after a tea-time break, back to their chairs.
Last week, one of them told me about her husband
quitting Northern Ireland for Corby, the steelworks,
job security – that was her home for thirty years: Corby.

My son is about to have the time of his life,
condoms in the pocket of his kit,
skateboard strapped to it, to be ditched whenever.
An enormous wonder
is about to unfold, starting on Wednesday.
He holds her hands. His voice is close.
What's this thing he's going around?
'You just enjoy yourself,' she says.

Her chin jerks down in a jolt of sleep.
She can hear voices, ours in the room, on TV.
Her eyelids lift then settle into a drowse.
Soon she'll be left in complete darkness
in a carefully dug hole behind railings
along the road by a bus stop, noise of traffic,
just lightly encased in the vibrations,
her head inclined as it is now,

hands hooked together,
going through whatever will be gone through
to the next ice age,
long before which the voices will have stopped.

ETC

Watching a friend half-way down a lane
turn back suddenly, you said –
'She's misbethought herself'. *Misbethought?*
remembered something, gone back for it,
got it wrong then put it right,
it's not this way it's that. Etc.

Etc's one of mine. It can be added
to anything, small or large –
Curtains, etc. Marriage, etc,
Meaning *know what I mean well more of it*.
But I'm wondering what your Misbethought
thinks about my Etc, etc.

Your loss of so much memory,
my lack of anything to remember
except that five years ago you misbethought
yourself while I kept going on and on
into more of the same.

HIGH DEPENDENCY WARD

Three a.m., on and on, like the scrub of a brush,
his cough loosens his wound from the inside.

Now three thirty, the hospital generator,
enough charge to drive a city, switches power
thud thud from the grid to the wards.

                        I just listen, can't sleep,
bolted to pain all night, plugged to the half-light.
But him over there, where the nurses swerve and stand
around his bed, concerned –
'Brian, use your mask. Come on sweetheart',
hurls it as far as he'd like them thrown.

Four o'clock, they call in help. Without oxygen,
a heart stands as much chance as a pound of fish,
exclaims the surgeon using technical terms,
'And… if I'm called here again, you'll be sorry'!

Four thirty, it gets worse, mask hanging off
having it his way, what can they do?
Change his sheets, his catheter, wire him back
to the instruments (temperature, blood pressure) –
he's just pulled out, self-powered!

Weeks till yesterday his heart was in a sack-race,
now with its goggles, engine and rider, trying to jump
out of his body, now a triple-necked amphora
pouring its new wine.

But all he wants is a ciggie: 'My rights!' he shouts,
eye to eye with the most predatory nurse
who can take blood, lunges at her.
'Don't touch me like that, Brian'.

Fumbles his way out of bed, twice in a night unplugs
himself from the wall, (he's coming over – am I next?)
rage revving his cardiac muscle, free of state control.

Five o'clock, quiet, under a blanket, his curled-up form
squeezes a cough, another. I'm gazing out
at steam from the power station,
pale blue daylight flooding Leeds.

BLUE FOOTBALL

The blue football floats on the green river.
Downstream. It has no choice.
It is happy to be this way up.
Or that. It doesn't matter.
It has been kicked out of reach.
Stares under itself, stares up.
No one is running to save it.

It's in its element now.
No one can climb on board.
It sits in the palm of the current.
Fields can pass or a garden.
Gentle rapids make it revolve a little.
Is that a crime? It doesn't care.
Whatever, it says. Whatever.

Will you marry me? Whatever.
Are you about to be recycled? Whatever.
It is a sunny day I think.
I float in it. Green river.
Arrowy leaves, pale ripple barbs.
When I bounced into this place, I adhered
immediately, like we were meant.

What a kick!
I'm not like you, little girl.
You, slimy rock. Or you, rapid dazzle.
The blue football floats on the green river,
sings to itself up and down, up-down.
Some things stay as they are.
The moon for instance

bobbling over the deep.
I thought I'd be safe with nobody.
Not long until some child though,
some terrible child – etc, I know it.
Blueness and shine they love, and joy.
Blue and wet together – how I float.
They will put their arms around me.

ALGIERS

You can meet Camus on the beach,
but don't look into his eyes, don't show
you're carrying a pistol, don't mention his mother.

An intensity in the distance like a sandstorm
is the news of plague in the next city
arriving by motorbike.

The food's so spiced it tastes of pinemartens
grilled with pilchards, so hot it burns your feet.
There's a restaurant where the flies are cooks.

The men and women of Algiers
are on good terms. Which language
do you sleep in? is a valid question.

The dead come out in the streets at night.
They stand about discussing Descartes, Derrida.
From them rises a sound like rattling stones.

CALIGULA'S RULES FOR GOVERNMENT

The fourth Caesar should have been Drusus
or Germanicus, but you happened.
You grew up with Tiberius's vague
melancholy as guide.
It made you specific in your design of pain.
Those suffering anguish are delicacies.
Crush them, keeping their hearts alive.

Games held only at night, torches ablaze.
Your poetry contest winners licking their slates clean.
The serious way you took your aspirations –
Become a god but one whose whims
outwit all sane reckoning.
Find the vein where pleasure runs,
quicken the circulation, then strike.

Uncertainties of impermanent indecision
 excite terror. Sword-flash
of your headsman at the wedding
when everyone thought you slept,
a nod and the groom gone, the bride yours.

Not a whisper between Thought and Act.
Not just to say, 'I can do anything',
but doing it. State brothels
where a round-up of wives and sons
of the arrogant classes serve everybody,
attendance compulsory, revenue
to the Emperor's stuffed purse.

Rules in reverse, or more to the point
government by surprise, chancy as war,
your own death the one predictable thing,
popular, theatrical, but its clumsiness
so unrehearsed, leaving yourself behind
as part of the mess to be cleared up.

BACKSTAGE, KING LEAR

Rows of pikes, banners, crowns and chains,
stocks, sacking cut in holes,
a large map-topped table.

Piped water trickling from filters.
They've tested it and it rains.

A mandoline – What's that doing? Is there a song?
The prospects are not good.

Gloucester's chair, and some contraption
of iron, waiting its cue, riveted black,
a bandage torn and bloody, or a blindfold.

It's going to be tough
in this world where everything has a purpose.

WOMAN WITH A JACKDAW

Apart from this one adornment gripping
her wrist the sitter is naked.
Sleek, swart,
cocking its head,
soon it will let go,
flutter the room, strut the floor
knocking the bare boards,
too much sense to fly at a closed pane.

Delicate,
claws thin
as an eyelash,
ghostly, reminiscent,
its glance a stab of black,
head feathers so soft and flush
it could be fur she touches,
feeling the grip on her wrist
like fate but temporary.

It caws, loud.
Everyone laughs.
She smiles, shakes her head at it, a gesture
it imitates, or seems to.
The moment passes.
It flaps away, does its strutting.
It will be gone in days,
over the gardens,
the woods shaped for November,
where to be out of sight is to be lost.

DIANA AND ACTAEON

Sometimes when she sees him
it's like the first time –
when the veil lifts and she knows
if she doesn't somehow quickly

change him into a stag
for his hounds to tear to pieces
he will tear her to pieces.
At our kitchen table I see,

as in the painting, the right shoulder
and raised arm of the hunter
as he looks towards Diana, the girl
he sleeps with, passing her the butter.

The strong, hair-flecked brown arm
of Actaeon, and surprised, helpless,
the sleepy face of the goddess
on New Year's Day afternoon.

MONET IN BRADFORD

1906, snow on the tracks,
the London train leaves Bradford,
platform and station edged like shapes of fog.

Proud Bradford with its London connection!
The train pulls out as two men shovel snow
trapped by black carriages going off-screen.

Monet was never in Bradford unless
you think of the place as a mood, an affliction,
as when his wife on her deathbed
lay in her own deep twilit freeze,
encased in a blizzard of gauze
in the drawing he made of her,
poverty a sharp icy draught.

A magpie on a gate on the path to the village,
thick snow on the fields like roughened plaster.
Affliction becomes lit. A low sun, just out of sight,
softens the breaking ice downstream from Paris.

Light moving south has started to melt.
There are bathers under the trees by the rowing-boats,
children with garden sunflowers, pots of golden-rod.

And in the stations, trains with long funnels
shoot out steam like coral feathers.
Huge pistons slide, and streets of people,
crowds at dusk where apartment lights
multiply into a million points,
feel spring engaging, its volume increase,
Le Pont d'Europe   out out
Gare St Lazare to the world.

Monet paints   His oils are a vital sign.
But Bradford is still Bradford.

I re-run the footage. The train leaves.
Two men shovel snow dusk freezes colourless.

SATURDAY BELLS

Keen to see them off to a good start,
outside the cathedral a crowd gathers
as a new bride arranges her veils,
her creams, the sky full of chimes,
disappears to be married.

The bells have crashed into silence.
Crows make their regular tree-top noise.
A fighter jet is invisible somewhere.
Tyres occasionally rip by on cobbles,

while for those inside, enclosed and hidden,
each shuffle, echo, every cough,
his voice, hers, saying 'I do'
to the creaking of pews,
sharpens their hearing,
lost in such uninhabited spaces.

The bells wait for the words, 'I pronounce…'
then raise the roof, hurl out celebration.
We feel it like a storm, a change of pressure,
sounding from cathedral towers,
topped by moors and Pennine sky.

Guests spill out in grey, mauve, yellow,
down the street in buttonholes, hats, high-heels,
two in Sainsbury's joining the lottery queue,
one by a shelf of champagne.

Bride and groom alone in a hired white Rolls
try to feel the transformation,
'Is it real… forever… Can I tell?'
'Let's hear it,' shout the bells,
'for the laws of Love and Chance,
two people changed by having met'.

RUBBISH

In WOOD AND TIMBER, a sideboard under pressure
of knuckle-duster spikes starts to explode.
It's been wanting to do this for years.

In SCRAP METAL, strange marriages –
ironing board with Flymo,
John Smith's cans with padded garden recliner.

From PLASTICS the word Organic tilts up.
Also Lenor, Diet, Cravendale, Piz Buin.
Every name means empty.

At TOOLS FOR AFRICA, I lift a lid.
Three handsaws and a bitless drill.

Our now permanently empty fridge
stands in a corner clinically depressed.

In BUILDERS RUBBLE
this slim white ceramic pedestal
has no future but hardcore.

Some things, never to be recycled,
envy the crash of glass.

On top of NEWSPAPERS AND MAGAZINES
The Story of Evolution, David Bellamy,
Edwina Currie's *She's Left Home*.
desperate to be pulped.

In the yard over a fence, cars, trucks,
once all shape and future, now piled high,
swing in a pincered grip.

BEACHCOMBER

Sometimes a concrete block, an iron pulley,
frayed rope attached like hair in a fist
selects him from the thousands who walk here.

Anxious about extremes he considers
how miniature mainstream estuaries
spin out a theme of glass, transparent architecture
of prisms, fine sand.

Over echoing heaps of stones he strides looking
for non-stories, ordinary relics,
cuttles, claws, pie-crusts with small eyes.

He heaves up rocks happily knowing
he will see no faces there, no weapons.

Once he found a swollen paperback
open at its spine like a Japanese fan,
the words sea-scrambled, unintelligible.

He took it home –
proof that the elements say nothing.

THE HACKFALL DRAGON

Traffic on the M1 snakes and glitters
but the only far-off sound is the river
here where land folds into deep gorges.
I can see down through almost the whole wood
where birdsong scatters.
Beech roots on a rock ledge
wrestle with their own strength.

February afternoon sun
opens the wood to space
among branches, twigs riding the sky.
Dens of bracken are smashed, and now
down there is something like bronze treasure,
freakish gold. What marvel is this
in the Hackfall gorges?

I stop half-way on the trail down,
still can't find the source of it,
then see the hill opposite, pyramid-shaped,
shining into the river, scaling it over.
A hill of fiery trees in the fierce light
changing wetness of rock, channels,
pools, currents to gold.

Seen through threadbare spaces
a dragon of water, slipping out of water
into metal, from what happens –
as it happens – to memory,
never simply river this time of year,
changed by daylight's alchemy,
continuously catching fire.

THE WILD HUNT

Riding home from the wedding of Elfland's king,
the flanks of their horses shone like hot brass
as they crossed the Usk towards Wye.

Three hundred years in the space of three days
had changed the gates of their holdings into woodpiles.
Hardly more than a burial mound was left.

The skull of a shepherd gave them the news.
Those who talk to spirits at the edge of darkness
come back with only themselves for company.

One cried out, 'The dead speak from the future.
What would those in our time have given
to look through our eyes now!'

Another remembered flames in dry pine,
the haunch of his wife's shadow,
his sons, Kynan and Adeon, playing chess.

Unable either to hold still or go back
all of them rose in the air. Hooves trampled the wind.
One who tried to dismount was dust instantly.

WONDERFUL LIFE

1

Transparencies with eyes,
frail hatchlings, a spirit-cloud
drifting across the rocky crust
of the earth to cling there,
but stone's the argument.
Chalk, shale, lias
invade, displace
lizards mica-scaled,
ripplings of crinoids.

The human's an appointment
not yet arranged, consciousness
still lodged in the gut of arthropods,
while man's, behind eyes,
in softness of self,
a to-fro eddying,
hasn't arrived. But
here he is, late, lost,
running to catch up.

He and she
and more and more,
all with a version of *now*,
and later *then*,
hardening towards
not what they once thought.
The future's another
story, and they'll never
hear the end of it.

2

On a mantelpiece certain things have collected:
a dice face up on three,
sweet wrapper, glass of unfinished orange,
scrap of white coral, sea urchin,
ammonite from Penarth,
a thing used to inject footballs with air,
bowl with scrapings of soup,
and this lamp conch,
horned helmet of a tiny wizard,
curved inside but otherwise ridged and extended,
could be a model of the complete shape
of space in the universe,
fifteen billion light-years rim to rim.

Yet this universe – however wonderfully
curved its fluted dimensions, unborn stars
in its nebulous hard wrinkles –
has no vicinity.
It is what we are not, it has no relations.
No seas feed their tides through the spiralled
in and out of a mouth tasting nothing of salt.

EDUCACION

A day's journey to our overnight camp,
two white hens in the bows for slaughter,
the outboard drives us noisily upstream.

The American in the stern gives an opinion
on what's killing the planet. 'The cow',
he pronounces, while air flow flosses cloud
around his head, blown fog covers each shoreline.

The wind is like spring in England. We shelter for warmth
in this tropic new to us.
From mid-river we can't tell if these
dense shores are banks or islands.

In an hour the cold evaporates. The sun bites.
On the boat's prow, my hand rests near the word *EDUCACION*
carved into hot wood.

A coastguard gunship passes. Not us they're looking for.

Near the shore, children are caught in the wake, heads swimming.
From huts on stilts, others run out, wave to the boats,
shin up trees, somersault in the water.
The river folds over them like oil.

Sunset flips into night. Banks of mud in a moment
are golden saliva. Floating trees,
pieces of earth like islands collide with darkness.

What I don't know is that three nights on,
back in Iquitos, in a long downpour,
I'll stand by the river, euphoric
in the rain's blessing –

and will give my thanks to the great spaces
for having come this far, my children with me.

I won't know, as the rain soaks me through,
that the next morning a sound out of nothing in the air
will change to a passenger jet coasting across New York,
then another, on our hotel TV.
We shall be watching it as it happens.

21/2001

> *"Your hair's all twisted, and you ain't speakin' right"*
> Leadbelly song

For Lucy

1

Across the street from Whitechapel tube,
dodging a shower, there it is, where you are –
after a call, *Dad, need to see you, they're doing tests…*
High steps, grand entrance, sun late September, still warm,
walls black as viaduct stone in the time of TB.
Then the lifts to your ward, cables coiling,
and there you are, smiling in your bed,
surrounded by friends, flushed with fever.
You're wanting to get up but feel too tired.
Your mother's there from another city.
I've some Peru photos with me, Get Well cards,
kisses from X and Y, not forgetting
the sixteen-year-old drinking tea on York station,
thin as a fox, telling me he's up for affray,
wishing you well too when I explained.
Round the next bed a Muslim family visit and old woman,
mother or grandmother: for a whole hour
not one says one word, wrapping themselves
only round each other, as if – they might think –
this place exists to cure them of themselves.
Distempered walls, people packed in like a street,
lines of public beds, ancient mouths trapped open,
sleeping or unconscious. We talk and talk, silence
from the next bed seeping through
as we stand up to leave still talking.

Next time I'm with you in hospital it's three weeks later,
north, near home. Home is where you want to get
but they won't let you out. Two ward orderlies restrain you,
your mouth stuck wide in a kind of shout. The door between us
swings to. Through the glass I see you dragged
further back in, told to behave. Nothing I can do.

2

The sports section interests you more than the latest attack.
You read that too, dangle a hand to the fire,
fold a page, stroke the cat at your elbow.
Home from college, convalescing, none of the doctors
knows what's wrong exactly. All you need is rest.
Soon you'll be back with friends, voices, laughter, essays, classes.

You just sit reading the paper, then stop, put it down,
grab my hand, smile What were you reading?
'Nothing' you say, 'none of it makes sense'.
I look at you – serene, vacant. Heat from the fire is it? Or what?
What?

I go shopping. Something's wrong.
I register this casually, notice myself stare
at litter of leaves and cracks in the path. It registers –
this is new, yet not like anything needs to be done,
not for circulation, still as if a gust might blow it away.

3

In PC World a boy your age shows us the state of the art
in this latest laptop. He's your business.

You're tired, so I push you round in an office chair.
You and he keep on connecting, connecting,
he, cool, professional, entranced,
hair spiked like an atomic kitten.

In a surround of screens you interview him,
What's he paid? In debt you bet. Social life.
Enough or not? Who's in? Who's out?
You talk the talk, topping the line-up,
instant access over a coffee on the house.
You're tired, but the whole shop's a party.

                Days later I call him.
We won't need a computer. You are ill,
seriously now. Did he notice anything strange at all?
He says no, most of the kids he knows act like that.
It's what we do, but sometimes I think, Christ...

4   *After Peru*

After talking with you in the canoe
slipping through rivers in the Amazon forest
about the age of our species, when suddenly
scattering down through scattered trees
people ran to the shore from their village,
young men and women your age, sharing
your century, yet dark and isolate in the vastness
like an illustration in a book. After the High Andes
where our guide took us to meet his friends
in their hovels, bringing loaves
for children still at school in the upper air,
red of serapes and caps drinking the oxygen.
After the beautiful herdsmen catching a lift
down the ravines, dry gulleys for roads
in our transit. Red sharpened by September ice
across peaks, inches under the soil.
After the catacombs in Lima,
waiting our flights, the departure lounge,
you through Amsterdam, we through Newark,
walking around the airport shop as if anything was nothing,
at the café table you said goodbye, held me in your arms,

yet I knew – about to watch us climb towards sky-fall
and its crater, you had inhaled the dust of the collapse.

5 *The President of England*

The day you woke up unable to find words,
only repeat, *What's going on dad?*
I took you to a doctor; he thought cannabis
could have got through the membrane softened
by meningitis exhaustion into your brain,
that it would pass (maybe).
Then having tried all day to bring you out of it,
I drove you that afternoon to A & E.
Could you count back from 100 in 3s? (you could).
Did this mean you would be granted asylum
in the land of the sane?
Not necessarily, we would have to wait.
'And who is the President of England'?
asked the locum, a young German, handsome
with a concerned nonchalance when we laughed,
and an am-I-supposed-to-know-these-things smile.
'Come again', you said to him, 'get real'!
So we pronounced you *you* and brought you home.
Two days later your mind slipped from its ledge
down, down. We took you in, screaming for life,
for your newly emerged adult life,
twisting and furious. 'This is the only way
you'll get it back', I shouted, delivering you
to the doctors for days, maybe for weeks, for life.
It was your twenty-first birthday.
In just days the Presidents of England and America
launched their attack and search, while the terrorist
hidden in his folded mountain cave
kept to himself the map and the legend.

6

she sits on the floor
she stares at her empty hands
the one she can't close
which has somehow been told not to close

she stares into this permanently open hand

while the other flexes grasps

opens
        closes

but the other will not even move

she sits on the floor
staring into the opening closing hand
operative of her will
into which reality will not fall
and the other into which it will

7

The hotel pool in Iquitos, rusty, deserted,
then, that morning, walking together from the foyer
along a street where men in shirt-sleeves
sitting with typewriters lined the pavement –
typing what? We didn't know, but as we speak
this is now our version of the ordinary.
You want to be exactly like that again,
just as you were then, in that street.
'You will', I say. 'You will. You can do it.
Just hold on, hold on. It will come'.
Sitting up close to you in the ward
your brother shows you a book, *Trail of Feathers* –
how the vanishing Incas discovered flight

long before Columbus discovered America.
'Read it', he's saying, 'read it to the Consultant.
'Tell her about it. Tell her about Peru.
Then she'll know you're cured'!
So you practise reading a passage aloud,
understanding nothing. It's just words.
'This is what I've got to do – read this? Then she'll let me go'?
He shows you a shaman holding a jaguar's skull.
'I was there', he tells you, 'I held it – this skull,
exactly as in this photograph'.
He talks about what matters to him most,
conjuring the jungle through his voice,
as if he, your brother, were your shaman,
as if you might stagger into flight.

8

From the hospital after a bad visit,
my son and I take the road to Brimham Rocks
on the moors above Pateley.

For ten thousand years, a slippery wind
has made no impression on stone that showed
no sign of retreating.

Here we were safe. If we could stay up here,
if the sun could somehow not come back –

It did us good to drive without speaking
in that ice-age land.

9 *Hijack*

Against the part of her mind that goes on repeating:
I love you all, you my brother, you my father, my mother,
hugging us, folding our hands into each other's hands,
we say No. Stop that. Listen while we talk to you about

football, fishing, the garden, the cats, anything,
even the news. Gripping us, she repeats, I love you,
remember, like a voice making its last call.

10

She talks to the boy who tells her when he's cured
she will inherit his illness next, that just by
speaking to him it transfers.

She tries to read *Atonement* which her girlfriend
has given her for a present, but the force of the word-tide
drags her slowly away with no rescuer.

Now she rehearses walking across
the polished surface of words, without taking her eye
off her mind, just in case it slips into a corner,

lies on the floor, might not get up again.
At which point she shouts, runs shouting. *I'm alive.*
Let me out alive!

11

Deep in talk with another patient,
a woman three times your age,
there's something you want me to know, and quick –
You pull me to the middle of the room,
sit me down facing you at a table, grip my wrist.

'Dad, I'm telling you straight, I'm bent'.
I don't get it... not at first.
'Yes, that's why you're here,
so they can help' (something like that).
'No' you say, 'We're an item...Me and J'.
The woman who'd been talking to you brought us a cup of tea.
'You've told him, sweetie? Now you'll be alright!'

Of course it's alright. Bent... straight?
I have no way of measuring you but love.
I say as you go to the phone, 'Give J my love'.

The energy packed inside you as you ran
back to your room to pack your bags and run,
your mind lost in itself, your illness glittering.
'I've told you so I'm cured so take me home'!

12

You in a chair, feet bare,
keep on plucking from your jacket
strands of very long blonde hair.
Your phone rings, you can't speak.
A friend is saying *Hello Hello*
to someone hanging upside down in the air
staring at them through a window.
They won't know it's you gripped by the heels.
you with your voice shaken out of you.

13 *Fame*

At the ward window,
looking out on a distant digital repeat
of cars on a road, she sees them jammed
in traffic behind glass, all technologies tuned
into dead channels. Faces,
cages of fingers around gears.
Their mouths coming ajar
in tiny laughter, visible groans,
every personal life a storm of holes,
each with its compact, folded problem
opening in acclaim – *Save us. Save us.*
You are the One with the Call.

The sun behind ragged dawn coverings

reveals its unreal kerosene-devilish light.

(You are the One!)

She stands at the window
open at its most three inches,
thinking what fame dares.

She hears them singing –
Free yourself. Free us!
their morning siren call.

14 *Double portrait*

When you seemed so much yourself
too much to be inside one skin –
she appeared, an excess of you
that must fly, like a Chagall spirit
out of the side of your head in yellow and white
like the blurred, fiery tail of a comet.

Most people in their twenties
have lovers and two heads.
There are hands meeting in mid-air
doves, violins, a tambourine.
It's your voice I think where difference lies
joined at the head, same hair, same eyes.

Or it's a girl with her ABC,
learning to talk, to draw and paint –
What would I give for a conversation
nobody interrupts with her no-answer,
her repeat question? Can't we slip away privately
you and I, so you can tell me what's going on?

A donkey and sunshade, all one to me,
people in yellow flying away,

and cellos and horses.
How much she produces!
One whole face next to its half-other
upside down in the moon's place.

I'm so tired of starry design,
angel and acrobat, cockerel and clown
eyes in the wall of a house.
What do *they* see?
What's *her* take on it all? Tell me!
A man with his head cut off at the mouth.

15

Every morning the shock like new knowledge
after deceitful sleep. I walk through the ward, meet you,
give you a hug. You're talking too fast again.
'Shall I read you something'? I say, to calm you.
I remember reading you, as a child, Blake's *Tyger*.
It gripped your soft bones.
Now on the hospital shelf *Love and Friendship*
Alison Lurie. I start it. Neither of us are interested.
I try Clive James's autobiography. Dull totally.
'Take your pullover off', you say, 'it's untidy.
Can I throw it out of the window'?
You walk to the half-open barred pane, drop a piece
of tissue-paper into the hospital courtyard's outside air.
You remember how I plaited your hair
in Peru in the heat. 'You did it so well'.

I go on reading. 'Can I put your pullover on?
It's cold. Go to the loo'? 'Yes. Yes'. So you go.
You come back in your trainers, in my pullover.
Then you run, along the corridor, down the stairs,
through swing doors, the foyer, into the street.
You are an athlete. It's October. Sunlight slants

over the end of working-day traffic, and I'm running out
in the day. In the road. I look for a figure
in my red-green pullover. This way. That. No sign. Then I see you.
You've torn it off between the cars, flagging this one down,
another, shouting at drivers, *Take me home!*

I catch you, drag you towards the grass,
hear your shout, *Let me go. Who are you?*
I don't know you! as if cut from the frame.
I had your wrist in a never-let-go grip,
and your hair, in a wad, in my fist,
behind your back, as if twisted by hands
of some orderly, to whom this was just a routine
psychiatric incident in the traffic.
They came eventually and retrieved us.
A nurse with her fingertips on your case
sat with us in a room.
For minutes I couldn't speak.
It was you who reached out.
You were the one holding the broken one.

16   *Internees*

Not so much trapped in undergrowth
as in machinery used to cut it down,
there are woods they should be out of now.
Your illness rolls back your eyes, makes you laugh,
won't behave when it's you we've come to visit,
nor will the others, Jenny's voice shouting
Ma-ad Fu-ucking Cow on and on at somebody.
There's a wall the upset girl slides down,
somebody on about his beautiful wife,
a messenger to himself, gratified with conviction,
about how she's waiting for him out there,
and the crossword, inked by a hand that
for every clue writes BECKHAM.

17
I bring her some presents to say she's getting better…

I carry them – a little packet of herbs for sleep and calm,
ginger for heat, along the wide corridor to her room.

But the expression on the face of a nurse
turning a corner towards me
is empty of reassurance.

Sometime during the late afternoon walkabout in town
she's escaped into the folding night.

This time she's already hours away.
The worst is a big step closer.
I stare at the cover sheet on the hospital bed.
Until she's found I can't move.

They tell us the police have been informed.

18
That moment when the people in the plane ripped in half
in the mountains realise there's no help anywhere,
fuselage buried in hopeless ice, their food supply
bodies of friends in the starlit freezer.
Or when the path into dead-end woodland
leads to the beast that eats and no one comes back. Worse,
when you know it isn't a movie, not a rehearsal, isn't a take.
Nobody directs. It's not even a story, but you're in it,
in *something*. Better any horror than this – the empty bed,
folds of cloth, unoccupied room, pointless door.

And when, after the phone-call saying she's safe,
that a friend has found her, is looking after her,
that she'll arrive soon with the police,

when I'd recovered some use
for my eyes, and she was there in the room, she didn't smile.
She could see that I was livid with relief, ratty with it,
with her, the nurses, consultant, things at random,
the colour of the wall. Rage, then calm –
a feeling I could almost ignore, play with like clay,
sculpting it, or, like cork, just let it float away.

19

Here you can't cross a street to get away
from the guy who screams at people outside Woolworths –
can't not know his name since he knows yours, is standing here
in the ward with you. And one whose hand you held
when you were twelve, now plays patience
while you watch TV, on and off all afternoon
in the smoke-room. Your mind, you thought,
could be infected like skin, their dread,
their terrors becoming yours by a touch, a word.

But now as the smoke
of your cigarettes and theirs
hazes the room, your mind clears.
This young man of fate with a sense of outrage,
this girl who apologises for everything –
you can be inside each one's story,
come out, go back in again.
I remember glimpsing you through the glass door
of the smoke-room –
what I saw there were signs:
you talking to them, they to each other,
your face turning to one then another,
listening, making them laugh.
She'll miss them, I thought, when the sane world
takes her back to itself, these others still on hold.

20

Bits and pieces of thoughts
through the scanner
brain sections like masks

neuroscience
can't do this repair.
It's how you read us, read yourself.

You know us but we don't make any sense.

neither do doors, bedroom sinks,
faces, windows, glasses of milk,
beeches losing leaves,

voices jammed like traffic,
single words   stalled there

moments and days, scattered
vital connections, now weeks.

                        Then one night
standing just inside the door
of the room where I write this,
two of your friends
tell me they've seen you.
'She's good… We've talked…
she's almost…' They daren't say it,
then the next night your brother
with the same report,
next morning the ward manager's voice
on the phone… Yes Yes (it's true)

by-ways of you strange but getting there
you are the one who comes back

Spring in winter, impossible news

as when

after such cries and half-lost hope
the dead are mended   the starved supplied   the disappeared found.

21

Twenty one in two thousand and one,
after days of long anxious inconsequence,
you getting better again then worse,
this was new: so many signs saying
to us you're here, and late in November,
driving towards the moors one afternoon,
my hands at the wheel turning glooms
of walls and hedgerows light in the last sun,
a field stood out, wrecked, luminous,
in the fold of a wood. A diamond
at the edge of the dark. Almost dark yet clear.

CLIMBERS AT WINSPIT

I wasn't there that day so have to imagine it,
his voice taut as the rope he holds from below
telling her to breathe slowly, relax,
concentrate on the next upward move of her right foot,
but her mind has locked onto the fact
that the world's too vertical, she must fall.

Summer. The sea moves in its blue quadrant.
The grass with its many tiny masts
lolls at anchor at the top of the climb.

And the climbs in her brother's book have interesting names –
Insanely Yours, Tom's Patience, Ride the Lightning –

His voice goes on and off like a lamp,
echoes round and round the corners of quarries.

She feels it guide her fingers to ridges and holds,
helping her to sample their jug hollows.
She has to make a move, now, now,
before it becomes obvious she can't.

The surface is there to help her, he tells her,
as he himself is there.

All this bright daylight in her head –
she wants to sleep while the breeze of time
adds more rock to the heaps below of fallen sea-smashed pieces.

He knows she must communicate now with the immediate rock,
close to it as a shadow.

All to scale and in easy reach
is a ledge the height of a knee.

She remembers the time five years back
when toe-holds, fault-lines, callused places
were out of reach, impossible,
a world of no way through,

herself
helpless, above and below confused planes of sheer vertical rock.

                  She clings
to his voice then lets go, lets drop
behind her its love, its instructions,
feels inside her own strength
how much lift is to be gained
from one firm press and swivel of force
down through the sole of a foot, as turning
on it she swings her whole body –
up up, hand over hand,
in rhythm, in mid air,
now at the summit, hovers there
surrounded in blue, abseils down
at last at last to a bright steady place.

WHAT WE LOVE

the shed by the river   a fire
hungry for wood chips on the hearth
candles all-over in stages of melt   hands
and faces with cards   Cheat   Motor
elbows and knees touching   shuffling
into more comfort   wine-glasses
emptying   filling

time just leaving us to it   warm pine
and the stove's metal heat   laughter
an outbreak of new flame   the shed
a wagon in a wagon train   the night
we went out   a meteor shower
its trail-blaze across wilderness
on a shelf   fiction   Tom and Huck inc
dampcurled   rivers and sheds unlimited

outside there might be a bear

LONE STAR RIDER

> *Comet Hale-Bopp made its closest approach
> to Earth on March 22nd 1997*

A shrunk and burning ice age with a tail,
rustling through the haze of constellations,
expected always to say something significant,
I am just an arrow that points at time,
I am just an arrow that points at nothing.

In range of you, everything becomes human.
I have to be careful of that because quite soon
I must return to the blackness without words,
not come too close, remember where I'm heading,
not be distracted. Believe me you are distracting.

You don't understand the clear light of amazement
through which I look down at the earth of ploughs,
after the earth of stones, the earth of grass,
after the molten rivers without ships.
Some kind of miracle has happened.

Maybe when I return you won't be here.
Nothing even conscious of you will exist.
I've seen no resemblance to you anywhere.
This might really be our last encounter.

My mind's iced up. I shouldn't be talking like this.
If only you could know how the intervals feel.
My head goes down so deep in space it freezes,
but not like any freezing in your vocabulary.
You don't understand time, you can't see it.
That's why you're so beautiful, so innocent.

Across you my trace flies, a short season.
I shall come back perhaps but species never.
A dead-centre sling shot to the forehead,
I could wipe you out, wipe you out.

THE HEAT AGE

1

Hand axes chipped themselves from flint.
Our story was cold.
                    The infernal wind
bowed over it, blew it out.

It lit again, with flamelike edge,
retouched, a hunting arrow.

Crossing the ice, fire scattered itself.

Our story was cold
but looking down from a remembered ledge
the glisten of ice was a lake.
Year by year the air seemed
to unfreeze, soften a little.

Alders grew by a stream where an animal drank,
a red deer from the forest.

I have to tell myself that I was there,
where standing frozen seas thundered.

2

Blue ice calved like steel from a furnace,
another story, not yet mixed with the human.

But fields dance, airs ripple, wheat begins,
a flow that will not cease under the wind.

Cold Great Bear becomes Warm Plough.

Our story is warm, moves in the mouth.
The gods of wood become bronze, iron, brass,

silver, gold, our doing, doing our will.
The god of stone is subdued to fluted pillars,
architraves, a devil perched on Chartres.

There was the story of leopard,
of rhinoceros. The red story of clay
painted onto the white story of calcite.

What was bird, monkey, snake, jaguar,
is now the story sitting by a window,
looking down on mud, magma, fire,
melting clouds, noise of in-drawn air, skin-burn
of the human, hot news, everything in its path.

3

Radiant with itself, the story,
cored from thirty thousand years,
tracks its warming, happening in no time.

At Altamira a child lifted her lamp, cried *Toros, Toros!*

while in a cluster of upright cloud
the sun behind a Ferrybridge smoke-mask
storms my mind, is slowly discoloured
by a huge slant of darkness.

                              The story
is underground, in the air, in the trees,
the sea like a skyline of land not going back,

is wherever I look, can't be dismantled,
forms impossible blocks, on all sides adamant.
No exit. Ourselves the heat of it.

THE FIRES OF SPRING

for Ruth Vicary

When it's winter,
and kids at bus stops
stand with no coats on
and red-ragged hands,
when overnight snow
is gone in the morning,
or lasts for weeks, piled in heaps
in car-parks, and the cheerfullest thing
is a self-checkout voice, saying
'Please take your change', we forget,
after the coldest winter in thirty years,
how brave and promising sunlight is,
how committed.

Up on the moors, some evenings in March,
fires make spaces for new heather.
Smoke lifts in columns over horizons.
Patches of dry ash are a war-zone smouldering,
Manchester in a Lowry painting,
little spurts of smoke from slum chimneys.
A silent tractor and men with long shovels
stand silhouetted in the soft orange burn.
Ice in the gulleys of soaked moor, smoke
turning the sun's disk blood-red.

On allotments, strange sheds,
held together by frames and nets,
bits of corrugated this and that,
signal their owners. 'It's time'.
Windy corners of dry cabbage leaves.
The soil too needs mending.

Over the beech-woods near Masham
a buzzard turns on a cloud-edge.
It cries. The whole sky
is an echo-chamber. Down avenues
of bare woodland, a pheasant
makes a sudden long-haul flight.

Our cat lifts his chin and seems to drink
the colour in the air.

At night starry Orion stands in the south.
Bright Venus hangs near the risen moon.
For a moment, by the foot of a farm wall,
a single cluster of snowdrops,
as if left there in memory,
glows with an equal fire.

VOTING FOR SPRING

> *Winter darkness brings on the extreme winter depression the Polar Eskimo calls perlerorneq. According to the anthropologist Jean Malaurie, the word means to feel 'the weight of life'. To look ahead to all that must be accomplished and to retreat to the present feeling defeated, weary before starting, a core of anger, a miserable sadness. It is to be 'sick of life' a man named Imina told Malaurie. The victim tears fitfully at his clothing. A woman begins aimlessly slashing at things in the iglu with her knife. A person runs half-naked into the bitter freezing night, screaming out at the village, eating the shit of the dogs. Eventually the person is calmed by others in the family, with great compassion, and helped to sleep. Perlerorneq. Winter.*
>
> Barry Lopez, 'Arctic Dreams. Imagination and Desire in a Northern Landscape'

1

Swanscombe on the Thames near Dartford tunnel,
a piece of occipital bone, the rest of the skeleton
powdered into cement for the Mulberry harbours.

Further north, England is Arctic.
We weren't going to be born for at least
twenty thousand generations, two more interglacials.

Still four hundred thousand years
before crocuses at their maximum yellow
splinter upwards out of the lawns of Hampstead,
sun on the lake warm enough for a swim,
from a hilltop the city.

Spring in the human
crossing the chalk ridges of Europe north
to valleys watered by Thames, to oaks and grass.

'What's the point?

You'll be dumped. Your future's a spoil heap!'

Something at the back of their long ridged skulls chose spring,
drove them forward through a door hinged
between the last and next devastation.

2

Ice drew its line in the far north out of sight.

Spring came but no people.

The sea lifted, carving a channel whose gorge
filled, sealing off Europe.

On the plain of York,
lion, rhinoceros, straight-tusked elephant,
grass the colour of fallow deer.

Sunsets glowed like the sun in resin.
Then the ice came back.

People wandered about on it looking for spring that when it
came would be recovery. Nothing happened.

They pulled the snowline over their eyes and ears.
They kept away from the sun, that deceiver.

Ice begins to engross them.

They run about in a wind that sucks the marrow out of their
bones.

Soon they learn to eat ice, trade with it, think it, speak ice.
They know they will die.
The thought warms them. They lie down in it.

3

Another people are standing close to the future –

The sun comes up, faint, like a hint of survival,
shining through generations.

They cover the tips of their fingers with red ochre from the floor of the Dordogne.

In the forms of deer, aurochs, ibex, a fleeting thing
emerges on walls of rock. Spring is with them.

4   *Dryas*

Out of the hollows of zero,
we made it,

a pestle, hoof-shaped,
milling the grain,

a reaping-knife
handled with the heads
of swimming deer.

                      From spears barbed
with flint, to pruning hooks –
'Let there be wheat', we said, and there was wheat.

Wild strains to stonewalled, cornered fields.
Amazement of green –

but horror of cold
persisted so deep
it swallowed us.

Here in the Northern hemisphere
spring came with its tundral dryas flowers.
Behind each small white petal were glaciers.

The cold returned just as we thought we'd made it.
Temperatures plunged headfirst into ice water.
                            A fragment of cold,
like a spear of ice, worse than the whole war.

By magic, by fires, by grace of the gods
from then on, we wanted a pact with the wind,
collaboration between ourselves and darkness,
a future in the organisation of storms.

Each year our fear was there,
horror of cold underfoot like an ice core.

Spring came, but by then we had other tools,
blast furnaces, power stations.
Now our coalition is with hurricanes.

5

Survival stops in its tracks, listens.

They hunt it down with generators, radar,
thermal imaging, statistics.

It hides in the wild woods. They check its prints,
think they have it trapped. It disappears.

The sight of their equipment exhausts them.
Decisions tie them up in savage knots.

The world looks like a ball in a string bag.
They drive clattering over the Great Plains.

Then they stop.

What reappears is a harsh planet.

Their future
is lichen under the ice where Spring forages,
hope written in cities.

6

Taking time away from the city, I drive to an area of woodland new to me. Along the path near a gate I find Fosters cans, a now faded and colourless Condor packet, a Hovis 'plain white' wrapper, a Kraft cappio cup, and in some brambles a big cardboard box marked Airmaster Tiger. A group of cyclists – some shouting to each other – ride past down the lane. A train rushes, must be through a cutting not far off. Noises from outside come and go with the same irregularity as cloud shadows; one recedes, another takes its place. Then for a few minutes the wood is silent. I hear a buzzard mewing high over trees. Birdsong returns. But these sounds don't interrupt the silence which has its own separate being. I move again. Here and there the path turns to swamp. Across the wood floor other wet and watery places appear. I go to investigate. A birch trunk falls away at one push, all compost. Leaves have turned to tar in the watery scum.

 This wood could be anywhere in the higher latitudes: big white fungi on trees, vines from last year's wild honeysuckle twined round fallen branches. One stump, still standing, is no more than a circular piece of bark, empty inside, wrinkled like the turret of a magic castle. I stir water with a stick. The surface twitches – with larvae, insects, spawn, or gas from decayed plants. The only obvious life, springy moss, might not survive another winter. Heat or cold could be killing the trees, or this apparent deadness might be natural. It seems chaotic but chaos could be its system: dead sticks, marsh, roots, bark. Then looking through the trees I see the faintest shimmering of green. The trees are producing, even in its merest, mistiest form, their first signal of spring: one the birds and insects recognise; one that says to us *engage, co operate.*

A few days later I enter another part of the same wood. I disturb a hare, which is soon out of sight. The wood's misty atmosphere has intensified, new grass in the marshy pools, some mosses pale yellow – almost white – others a deep viridian. For several minutes I stand very still, sealed in by trees. I am at ease, unmoving, part of the silence. Then I hear a noise, something like a very loud bark or a croak, the sound of a big animal at maybe twenty or thirty metres: again, then again, the sound of something huge, and close – a stag, a raven or a bear. I look up through the tree tops, then across. Nothing moves. The wood is all secrecy. A thousand curves, angles, twists, straightenings, hardenings and softenings. What hides there? I wait a while in the silence. Suddenly my phone is receiving a message: 'Struggling to get home from abroad and need help with your credit?' I give up listening, move on. A russety bumble bee nudges at ground level among the new honeysuckle leaves. A finch with a blur of colour flits overhead, the birdsong I'm hearing attached to it, or I think so. Other birds are singing further off. A woodpecker drums softly in the distance. In two or three days spring has happened, as it has done in this little wood for the past eleven thousand years. Everywhere is inhabited. I wander about, quiet as I can, searching for the animal with the call. I keep on, looking and listening, all the way back to the road.

7

Quite a performance,
that first sign on the apple branch,
days a soft urging.

No use staying put in the old house,
hot and cold like the voice of God
audible in the plumbing.

Spring needs spaces, planet-sized,
special to regions where disaster's gone on too long,
must be ended deliberately

if only we knew how, but we do. There are ways.
Courage. Belief. Then I hear cries.
For some Spring is away in another lifetime.

It can taunt, smile, still come to nothing –
be persuasive, almost, like the sound
of hammering in sheds.

What will become of it after the first hundred days,
after a year?

I see it crossing the Alps
in armies of fresh larch – the song
of the sun rumbling in the mountains,
doors on their hinges, sharp-shadowed,
opening to it or closing.

NATURAL HISTORY

Beasts in the cathedral   under misericords   on roof bosses
capitals   front-feet hooves   back-feet claws   wings
feathered or spined   an ape's little wooden testicles
headless men with faces in their chests   bagpipe swan
fox priest   elephant with the world on its back.

In South Kensington   a pterosaur   wings pleated
gazes at visitors in the queue by the porch   where I stand
below the museum's mock-Norman arch.   On walls   in niches
in the porch itself   carved terracotta storks   elk   lizards coiling
lars   lemurs   Milton's brutish gods.

The cathedral honours its war dead.   A tank is parked
the regiment's triceratops   maleficent   in the town square.
Broods of children climb its plated sides.
At the altar   a dragon with folded tail   a scaly horror
writhes skewered under the spear of St George

fixed in creation's six-day week   unable to grow extra
fresh thicknesses of defence.   The saint triumphs
continuously   the primitive put down.   The mammoth
in her lady-chapel in London is extinct   yes   but still living.
That elephant in the choir's hers   jaws   tusks

like ancient agricultural machinery   conversant
with the ridged skull of erectus.   In the central aisle
children's voices flutter between the bones of the diplodocus
head tilted   facing the door   as if the past   slowly put together
piece by piece   forests   seas   worlds of information

were visiting us   the whole museum claiming our attention
above road works   street noise   here to make space
for a new species of wonder   so that we say   I saw with my own eyes
earthrise   over the moon's sterile ranges   the one place where
living or having lived   so much belongs.

THE APPLE PRESS

Some rot from falling   skin broken
or bruise on the trees.   Most with a twist
drop perfectly into the picker's hand.

Some will soften   touched by others'
collapse   yet if decay spreads
a knife can catch it   there's time.

Then the pulper   industrial strength
its pitch hardly altering as they go in
toppled like heads   not too many at once

each one itself for the last time   rosy
blemished   notched   clefted   varieties mixing
in one spongy amalgam   peel   flesh   cores.

Then the press   first the muslin bag
then big leverage   circular clamp   oiled
threads   firm constriction   final

separation into the clear   dregs here
liquid there   Taste it   sweet sour   cold
thrilling.   And the day warm.

Dust in the yards.   Overhead
a cluster of rooks   cirrus threaded to wind
combed by force.   The air still here.